Table of Contents

CHAPTER ONE

IMMEDIATE EFFECTS OF THE PANDEMIC

When the COVID-19 pandemic had just hit Wuhan, China, the world had no idea that it would spread to almost every country. The impacts of the pandemic on the world permeated every facet of human endeavor. More than two million people have lost their lives globally, and more than 13 million active cases recorded.

When this started, we could never have imagined that we would last the whole of 2020 without an effective vaccine. But as the days passed and the nights passed, the world started taking the pandemic quite seriously.

COVID hit poor and weak nations the hardest, undermining many years of hard-won additions while compounding existing disparities in the most unfortunate countries.

The pandemic targeted homes, businesses, and families. The pandemic dragged a hundred and thirty million or more people into poverty, and the global economy experienced a gruesome recession.

Since then, governments worldwide have struggled to control the spread of infection and the rapidly rising number of casualties. A few nations have needed to force lockdowns and other safety policies to halt the pandemic's spread.

The pandemic caused many companies to adjust how they carry out businesses and address their staff and customers. In March, many companies turned employees' home, leaving the buildings of large industries that once had people coming in and out empty.

Large multi-national corporations that once bubbled with activities now had their facilities dry. The pandemic shut down so many businesses while other companies had their employees working from home.

All of this begs to question whether companies will continue to incur a considerable commercial office space expense. New employment practices have arisen with the shift to telework, from technology issues to basic employment practices.

As a result, businesses across industries were affected because there was a massive change in consumer behavior and spending. In the same vein, disruptions in the international supply chain have severely affected international trade.

However, the discovery of COVID-19 vaccines shows that the worst is over. In other words, the pandemic will soon be a thing of the past. Socio-economic indicators show that recovery is very much underway.

EFFECTS OF THE PANDEMIC ON MULTI-NATIONAL CORPORATIONS

As the pandemic spread through the world, it significantly impacted the movement of goods, products, information, money, and other factors of production between countries and regions. The implementation of national lockdowns and social distancing measures further aggravated the pandemic's effects on international trade.

Multi-national companies typically purchase raw materials from the cheapest sources, outsource work to countries with cheap labor, sell to high-income countries, and direct profits to low-tax areas. These companies' activities are facilitated by globalization and were adversely impacted by the spread of the pandemic.

The first phase is the impact of the pandemic on businesses. As a result of the drastic changes in consumer habits and behaviors, there was a decline in service consumption, car traffic, public transport use, and the urge to travel. Businesses in the retail, food service, and tourism sectors were affected the worst.

The travel bans and other safety measures' impacts led to a breakdown in global supply chains, unprecedented drops in demand and supply, revenue loss, and other operational setbacks. In a 2020 report on the impact of the COVID-19 pandemic on Foreign Direct Investment (FDI), the World Bank stated that more than 80% of all multi-national corporations had suffered some level of harm. Another study found that the top 5000 multi-national corporations have revised their earnings downwards by at least 30%.

In terms of travel, JP Morgan stated that air travel made up to 30% of multi-national corporations' budgets. So, they could cut back on travel costs and find ways to work around face-to-face meetings because of travel restrictions. Virtual meetings became the new normal, and many even began to wonder if face-to-face meetings were ever required to transact businesses.

In the same vein, the low-cost and easy set-up of virtual meetings caused the number of business meetings to skyrocket. Microsoft, for example, registered a record 2.7 billion meeting minutes one day in April of 2020. This figure was three times the average meeting minutes reported for March 2020.

Export restrictions have played a key role in limiting multi-national corporations' activities since the beginning of the pandemic. By May 2020, at least 85 countries had implemented some restrictions on exports to make up for shortages in their local markets. Several products, especially healthcare products, sanitizers, personal protection equipment, and so on, became the focus of these export prohibitions.

Tensions between the US and China reached frightening levels as they both imposed tariffs on the other's imports leading to a prolonged trade war. As a result, many countries will have to choose between the US and China moving forward. Many multi-national corporations will need to domesticate their supply chain and only produce goods for local consumption.

As vaccines become more and more available and the world begins the long recovery journey from the pandemic woes, distance-related barriers to multi-national corporations' activities will only become more apparent. However, this will accelerate digital solutions like remote work, virtual teams, augmented reality, and other technological innovations.

Multi-national corporations will have to revise their processes and quickly modify their strategies to respond to national policy changes (like Joe Biden's tax proposals), global competitiveness, and other pandemic effects.

For instance, risk assessment procedures will capture the risk of infectious diseases and reduce employees' need for travel. Multi-national corporations will need to localize their production processes to eliminate the reliance on foreign inputs.

They will also need to produce goods and services that will be consumed domestically due to export restrictions and prohibitions.

Most multi-national corporations will have to restructure to recover from the impacts of the pandemic fully. Restructuring, however, must be carefully thought out to reap its benefits fully. Restructuring does not necessarily result in massive layoffs.

Layoffs result in the loss of skilled workers and technical know-how. It seriously harms the affected workers, erodes the remaining staff's morale, and lowers the community's trust.

Instead, restructuring could mean training/reskilling workers, re-deploying staff, and in some cases, early retirement. It should aim to strengthen the company to survive the pandemic's effects, position it for rapid recovery, and increase its overall value.

In conclusion, while the pandemic brought a lot of hardship for multi-national corporations, it has also opened windows of opportunities to adopt new processes and success strategies.

EFFECTS OF THE PANDEMIC ON SMALL AND MEDIUM SCALE ENTERPRISES

Small and Medium-scale enterprises (SMEs) are the crucial backbone of any economy. These businesses account for 50% of global GDP and up to 70% of the world's employment. In the United States, SMEs are independent businesses that have fewer than 500 employees. They are prevalent in the retail, food service, transport, hospitality, tourism, construction, and other related sectors.

Historically, small and medium-scale enterprises have always been more vulnerable to any shocks to the economy. The COVID-19 pandemic was a testament to this as these businesses were hit hard, in most cases harder than the larger companies. The lockdowns, social distancing, and other safety measures that were put in place have seriously hampered these SMEs' activities.

A June 2020 study conducted by the International Labor Organization (ILO) surveyed 1000 SMEs from eight countries across four continents. The study reported that 70% of these companies had to shut down completely. Half of these businesses closed their doors due to government directives to curb the spread of the pandemic. The other half of these businesses closed because of a sharp drop in customer orders, staff infection, and other related reasons.

Almost 33% of the SMEs involved in the study reported that they had lost at least half of all revenue. They also were not expecting any significant improvements in the short-term as the pandemic continued to ravage across the world. They, however, expressed optimism for the nearest future but not without a bit of uncertainty.

From February 2020 to April 2020, the number of working business owners in the US dropped from 15 million to 11.7 million. The only industry that experienced an increase in business owners was agriculture. The 22% (3.3 million) decline was the sharpest drop on record, and the pandemic's impact was felt across all industries.

The construction industry lost 670,000 business owners within this timeframe, and how many of these will return a topic for speculation. Other sectors like retail, restaurant, and hospitality lost 10%, 22%, and 35% respectively between February and April 2020.

Other industries that were hurt by the pandemic include the transport industry. It lost 22% of its workers; the financial service industry lost 12% of its workforce. The professional/business service industry lost 18% of its workers, and the health service sector lost almost 16% of its workforce.

Statistics show that the pandemic hit African-American businesses the hardest. The number of black business owners dropped by a massive 41% between February and April 2020. Immigrant-owned business owners reduced by devastating 36% within the same period.

Businesses owned by Latinos were also severely hurt by COVID-19. The total number of companies owned by Latin-Americans dropped by 32%. The number of Asian enterprises also dropped by 26% within the specified timeframe.

Most SMEs displayed a similar response to the pandemic by immediately taking steps to protect their staff and customers from the infection. They kept their customers/clients apprised with updates as they came. Most also reached out to the government and other business bodies for support.

Some SMEs implemented retreating strategies like laying off staff, acquiring new debt, and even selling off assets to cope with the pandemic's hardship. Most other SMEs reacted by scaling down operations, shifting to online channels, and different strategies that would help them survive the harsh realities.

A handful of SMEs responded to the new reality with groundbreaking innovations, allowing them to flourish while others struggled.

The government acted swiftly to cushion the effects of the pandemic on SMEs. On 3rd March 2020, the Federal Reserve reduced the interest rate by half a percentage point. On 13th March 2020, the government announced that it would make $50 billion available as loans to SMEs.

On the 15th of the same month, they further reduced the interest rate between 0-0.25% to make loans more comfortable and more accessible for SMEs. Other government interventions include the CARES act that contained $349 million as interest-free loans for SMEs.

The government added that principal on the loans spent on utilities, rent, payroll, etc., will be forgiven if recipient small and medium-scale business owners maintained the same number of staff they had before the pandemic hit.

On 30th April, the government announced an increase in the volume of funds available as loans to SMEs. The amount rose from $349 to $600 million. Other states like New York, San Francisco, Illinois, and California also provided safety nets and financial aid for SMEs to cushion the impacts of the COVID-19 pandemic. Without these measures, more businesses would have inevitably shut down.

CASE STUDIES

The Coca-Cola company

The Atlanta-based beverage-making giant Coca-Cola was not immune to the impact of the COVID-19 pandemic. The multi-national corporation is one of the several MNCs that suffered huge losses and decline in sales as countries worldwide scampered to slow the spread of the virus.

The Coca-Cola Company entered into 2020 with significant momentum. Sales, as well as revenue, were at inspiring levels and until the pandemic struck.

The imposition of lockdowns, social distancing measures, and other safety measures led to a sudden drop in sales.

Restaurants, stadia, malls, and other retail outfits where consumers usually bought Coca-Cola products were closed. It caused the company's net profit in the first quarter to fall by 1% (to $8.6 billion).

In April 2020, James Quincey, the Coca-Cola CEO, said that the giant has become capable of surviving from its 134-year existence. He said 'every previous crisis; military, economic or pandemic - the Coca-Cola company has come out stronger.

With over 500 brands and more than 700,000 people under its umbrella, the company has had to respond to consumer behavior changes, market trends, and global supply-chain and distribution channels.

In August 2020, the company announced that it would have to restructure its workforce and lay off 4,000 workers globally (including in the US). It also reported that it would reduce the number of its business units to 9 from 17 units, and the nine will operate under four geographical segments.

The layoffs would result in severance expenses that would cost Coca-Cola between $350 and $550 million. The company enforced stringent safety precautions in all its facilities, implemented additional sanitization routines, and even restricted visitors. In many of its facilities, drivers don't even step out of their trucks.

Split shifts are also employed to prevent shift-to-shift contact. The company has also recommended that most of its office staff work from home to have no large gatherings and any form of travel, whether domestic or international. Coca-Cola has also spent more than $100,000 in its numerous community support programs.

Chaia Taco

Chaia Taco is a female-run small business that operates from two locations in Washington DC. The founders, Bettina Stern and Suzanne Simon are two phenomenal women who offer the most delicious vegetable tacos and drinks to customers all year round.

Chaia Taco is a 'farm-to-taco' shop which means that they get their vegetables (mostly organic) fresh from local farmers and combine them with spices and other ingredients to prepare the most delightful tacos.

They offer five vegetable taco creations, sumptuous sides, soup when it's cold, and various drinks that range from beer to tea to rosé. Consumers can customize their orders depending on their appetites or personal values too.

In March, when the pandemic had become widespread, Bettina said that sales dropped by a massive 85%. She explained that it was the most difficult time she and Suzanne had ever faced. The birth of the pandemic had thrown businesses and communities into unchartered territories.

On 15th March 2020, they had to close their shops down. In a bid to protect themselves, their staff, customers, and the community from spreading the virus. A few days later, the Mayor imposed a lockdown.

Bettina and Suzanne quickly adapted to the new norm by offering only pick-up, delivery, and take-out options to their customers. They also reduced their service hours and reduced the number of items on the menu. Another tactic was to split up so that one owner worked a shop with one employee. That way, they were able to adhere to safety guidelines and keep labor costs low.

The duo collaborates with local charities and other related organizations to supply food to healthcare workers on the frontlines against the virus. They believe that their flexibility and tenacity are what define Chaia Taco.

Moving on, Bettina and Suzanne said the experience had taught them that it is essential to go over the top to tend to the workers, genuinely support the community, stay vital, and stay relevant. They are grateful for their staff's cooperation and look forward to when everything is back to normal.

CHAPTER TWO

GLOBAL ECONOMIC SENTIMENT AND LONG-TERM IMPLICATIONS

The COVID-19 pandemic has shown that truly no man is an island. When it was first reported to be a health emergency in January 2020 by the World Health Organization (WHO), no one thought it would explode to reach this magnitude. In March 2020, WHO officially tagged it a global pandemic.

The first infection cases were reported in the City of Wuhan in China. The pandemic quickly spread to every corner of the globe. It is because of how interconnected the world has become. As the virus progressed, it spread to Europe, and within a few weeks, reported cases of infections in Europe reached one million.

It did not leave out the United States at all. The virus entered the US and began ravaging everyone/everything in its path. Like in every other country, the US's healthcare system was stretched to its very limit, with infected patients filling up hospital beds to the maximum.

In response to the spread of the COVID virus globally, countries began to put safety measures in place. Social distancing policies, isolations, and lockdowns became the new normal as governments scrambled to slow the infection rate. For most of 2020, more than 80 countries closed their land/air borders to people from countries with high infection rates.

As it stood in February 2021, the virus had infected more than 106 million people worldwide and claimed the lives of more than 2.3 million of them. In the United States alone, 27 million people got infected, and 464,000 Americans died due to the infection.

Governments have fought to slow the spread of the virus and remedy its adverse effects on the economy simultaneously, which has proved to be quite a daunting task. The safety measures like isolations, social distancing, and lockdowns to reduce the rising infection rate have caused economic activities to come to a stop.

In response, the US government (and its agencies) deployed several monetary and fiscal policies to offset the deficit. These policies were targeted at guaranteeing the flow of credit and stabilizing the financial markets. For instance, in March 2020, the interest rate was slashed in half twice, bringing it incredibly close to businesses' zero interest rates.

In the same vein, stimulus checks and other social security payouts were distributed to millions of vulnerable Americans to cushion the financial blow the pandemic delivered. Millions of households used the stimulus packages and other transfer payments to cater to the new pandemic lifestyle demands.

The International Labor Organization (ILO) reported that since the pandemic's onset in early 2020, the workforce lost more than 255 million full-time jobs worldwide. The ILO also stated that more than 93% of workers now performed their tasks under some form of workplace restriction.

In the context of the United States, almost half of the entire 160 million-strong workforce filled for unemployment insurance. These 77 million people filed for unemployment from March 2020 to January 2021. Most of them are approaching the 26-week maximum for receiving unemployment benefits.

They may be applying through either; the Pandemic Unemployment Assistance (PUA) program or the Pandemic Emergency Unemployment Compensation (PEUC) program.

The effects of the pandemic very terribly hit small businesses. Many small and medium-scale enterprises report that sales went down by 80% within a short window when the government-imposed safety measures, isolations, and lockdowns.

Customers stopped coming in as they had to stay at home, and many had to let go of some employees. In the same vein, between February and March 2020, the United States experience the sharpest drop in business owners. The number of business owners in America fell by 33 million, and these millions of business owners came from virtually all industries and sectors of the American economy.

The pandemic did not leave out Multi-National Corporations as the pandemic also hit them with record low sales and large disruptions in their global demand and supply chain. Big names like

Microsoft, Apple, Coca-Cola, and Guinness suffered significant sales losses and a decline in revenue.

These Multi-National Corporations have had to immediately adapt to the global business scene changes by embracing technological advancements and other remote work solutions. They have also had to restructure their processes to adhere to new safety guidelines while keeping business running near pre-crisis levels.

The demand for and supply of medical/pharmaceutical supplies has been a significant issue that arose as countries struggled to contain the virus. Personal protective equipment like nose masks, face shields, hand sanitizers, and protective gear for health care workers on the frontlines became scarce globally.

Pharmaceutical companies and other related companies who produce these items were instantly bombarded with orders. Countries had to vie with one another to supply the things that became a critical part of the fight against the pandemic. Some countries expressed their displeasure when richer countries were provided with these items because they were ready to pay more.

The frantic race for personal protective equipment continued into the race for creating a vaccine for the COVID-19 virus. Countries like the US, the UK, France, Germany, Russia, and Madagascar were among those who led the race.

Within the G7, the pandemic hit economic activity the most for the UK. The GDP fell by 20.4% in the second quarter of the year 2020, while the US's economy fell by 9.1%. The government reacted by including stimulus, but the stimulus was hardly a guarantee that any recovery will be swift. Everything depends more on the trajectory of the COVID virus.

Low-income countries had to go easy on the strict lockdown measures for the sake of the continuity of their economy and their citizens' health and lifestyle. Following social distancing rules and returned to work.

COVID-19 mortality is much higher in low-income groups, ethnic minorities, and older adults. Also, its economic effects are irregularly distributed across the world's population. The financial aftermath is probably going to be felt for quite a long time.

Without purposeful preventive measures, more impoverished families and networks will be lopsidedly influenced, expanding health and wellbeing inequalities worldwide.

UK had the biggest COVID-19 hit, but alarming health trends were developing in England even before the pandemic. The increased cased of child poverty, homelessness, and food malnutrition led to an unprecedented rise in child mortality, emotional health issues, and slowing life expectancy, especially for ladies in the low-income areas.

These were similar territories where ten years of severe measures had hit the low-income regions the hardest. More significant cuts in government subsidies to neighborhood specialists with greater extents of kids in poverty implied decreased spending on essential preventive administrations in zones where they were required most.

The pandemic showed up in the center of this stressful scene and enhanced existing disparities. Also, exposure to the disease is inconsistent. Individuals in dubious, low-paid, manual positions in the health, retail, and administration areas have been more presented to Coronavirus as they cannot do their jobs from home.

Overcrowded, low-quality lodging in highly-populated regions has added to their increased risk. The low-income group has likewise been more defenseless against severe sickness once tainted due to the previous disease's more elevated levels.

Expanded infection rates have prompted a more prominent loss of pay connected to disturbances to work and occupation misfortune. However, the quick monetary pressing factor of Coronavirus has gone a long way past this.

Control and lockdown measures have lopsidedly influenced low pay families with young children. Recent examination distinguished the additional costs of having kids at home for more without admittance to essential free administrations, requiring expanded spending on food, warming, and possessing kids inside.

Over 33% of low pay families with kids grew their spending during 2020, while 40% of high-salary families without kids decreased theirs. Rising interest for all-inclusive credit uncovered the deficiency of current degrees of advantages.

The UK government expanded all-inclusive credit installments by £20 a week to make up for additional lockdown costs. However, the expansion is just transitory.

Food poverty grew, with free school suppers—a fundamental nourishing lift for some low-pay families—being supplanted by crisis measures to forestall young kids going hungry during school terminations. Government upholds for this plan have been dubious, and on occasion, the efforts have been insufficient to keep up the soundness of developing kids.

Anticipated long haul monetary impacts incorporate loss of future profit and joblessness, pushing more grown-ups, especially guardians, into poverty. The effect of the pandemic on business is anticipated to be multiple times more noteworthy than that of the 2008 monetary emergency, which prompted a sharp expansion in suicides and mental illness.

The pandemic actuated downturn is probably going to have a comparatively harmful impact on emotional wellness. By a wide margin, the pandemic's most pulverizing long-haul expenses will probably fall on the present youngsters as they develop, create, and fashion their financial prospects. Child poverty is, as of now, the greatest danger to kid wellbeing.

There's been an improvement in the UK and worldwide, so the anticipated increment is unsettling. A mix of more regrettable monetary strain inside families and stay-at-home pandemic strategies makes mischief the turn of events and psychological wellbeing of kids, for more youthful youngsters relapsing in fundamental abilities.

As of now, one in every six kids and young ones have psychological wellbeing issues as their lives are "put on pause," with clear ramifications for their drawn-out wellbeing and profit.

Lost learning will best harm the capabilities and occupation possibilities of students who are now hindered. Requiring a "gigantic public strategy reaction," the Institute for Fiscal Studies assessed that missing a large portion of school time could mean losing £40,000 in lifetime profit, with negative impacts concentrated among kids from burdened foundations.

The basic outlining of activity as a compromise between ensuring wellbeing or securing the economy is a bogus polarity: worldwide proof shows that the infection should be leveled out for the economy to recuperate.

We need to shield the more regrettable off in the public eye from the unfriendly results falling lopsidedly on them, particularly by giving each youngster the best beginning throughout everyday life.

In the short term, this could incorporate holding the widespread credit inspire, raising the understudy premium, and acquainting concentrated measures with assistance impeded students get up to speed with lost picking up, including tending to the computerized partition.

In the medium term, the vast quantities of individuals jobless and those whose capacity to work are diminished because of the drawn-out impacts of COVID-19 will require compelling help and preparing to get back to work. Reinvesting in the youths' preventive administrations focuses and improved admittance to a scope of psychological wellbeing administrations will be pivotal.

Be that as it may, we should try not to introduce drastic measures to fix the economy, which would fall most challenging on the most impoverished areas and networks, enlarging wellbeing disparities, making the rich richer and the poor poorer.

CHAPTER THREE

2020 JOB CRISIS

Three weeks into the pandemic, the International Labor Organization (ILO) predicted that the new virus would threaten about 25 million jobs. In April of 2020, the latest dire assessment reflected the full or partial lockdown measures affecting almost 2.7 billion workers, which is 4 in 5 of the world's workforce.

That would mean that the COVID-19 impact on the world's economy will exceed that of the 2008-2009 Global Financial Crisis (GFC). Every sector of the labor force was affected, with workers in four sectors experiencing the most drastic effects.

According to ILO, 144 million workers in food and production, 482 million workers in retail and wholesale, 157 million workers in business services and administration, and 463 million workers in manufacturing sectors were the top affected sectors in the early periods of the pandemic.

They made up for 37.5% of global employment, and that was where they felt the bitter end of the pandemic's impact. Countries all around the world went into a worldwide lockdown. The effect of this was felt by most of the world's workforce. Everyone was affected. It included the G7 economies.

Various governments started to focus on protecting livelihoods and economically viable businesses, particularly in developing countries, by providing immediate relief to workers and enterprises.

However, in low and middle-income countries, where more than most of the workforce population were low-wage workers with limited access to healthcare services and welfare safety nets, the worst of the pandemic effect was felt. Without these appropriate policy measures, people were out of jobs in no time with no provision for stimulus or incentive packages.

Workers faced a high risk of falling into poverty and experiencing more significant challenges in regaining their financial stability during the pandemic period.

Around two billion individuals worked casually, the more significant part of them in arising and agricultural nations, and that "several millions" of casual laborers have just been affected by COVID-19.

In metropolitan territories, additionally, these workers likewise will in general work in monetary areas that not just convey a severe danger of infectious disease but, on the other hand, are straightforwardly affected by lockdown measures. These are the construction workers, waste recyclers, food servers, domestic workers, etc.

As we started accepting COVID as the norm, we started finding ways to get things done with the resources that were made available for us. People began working from home and did almost everything over the internet. Zoom video meetings took over the business interface as the pandemic hit. Workers from all over the world connected to their colleagues via Zoom.

Conferences, decisions, and execution of projects were mostly simulated and carried out between different people at their homes over the internet. Class sessions were held for students over Zoom.

Friends also, that had been forced to stay apart due to the global lockdown, often communicated and kept in touch via Zoom. Although this wasn't as effective as face-to-face communication, it was the next available best thing during the global lockdown.

Zoom became one of the most significant victors in the work-from-home universe of the COVID-19 pandemic, with shares up over 350% over the previous year. Whether this will continue when everything gets back to business as usual is unsure.

Some of the significant side-effects of COVID are unemployment and poverty, amongst other things. There was a $982 billion gap between the estimation of monetary stimulus packages and the damage done to the work market by the pandemic in poor and lower-income pay nations.

The ILO called for strategy intercessions to be made on a scale related to work market disturbances. Handling the role would require greater international solidarity, including debt relief and development assistance, which will be vital. The ILO also asked governments to guarantee that financial estimates reported are delivered rapidly and efficiently.

The inactivity rate is rising more rapidly than unemployment in every country apart from Canada and the United States. It is stressful and needs quick attention.

Only focusing on changes in unemployment can be misleading. Earlier crises have shown that activating the percent of the inactive population is way harder than re-employing the percent that was laid off, so higher inactivity rates are probably going to make recovering the jobs more difficult for the unemployed.

It includes the younger and older folks who have seen the dark side of the COVID-19 crisis. They are especially at risk because these two groups usually have a higher risk of becoming inactive.

Also, the latest data confirm that employment losses are larger for women than for men. Policymakers would have to target these main hard-hit groups, including women, young and older people, migrants, and domestic workers.

It should include continued income support and efforts to assist with workers' return to employment. The ILO wants to avoid large-scale and long-term marginalization from labor markets – ensuring that no-one is left behind.

The strictest form of lockdown – with required closures for all but essential workplaces across the entire economy or in targeted areas – is still in place for around 70% of workers in upper-middle-income countries.

Upper and middle-income countries implemented the strictest form of lockdown, with 70% of their workers still having most of their workplaces closed except for virtual workplaces across the entire economy.

Low-income countries, however, have relaxed their earlier strict measures, despite yet the increasing numbers of active COVID cases.

It is still crucial to get the right balance and timing of health, economic and social policy. Ill-advised or premature loosening of preventive health measures creates a risk of prolonging the pandemic and worsening its labor market impact.

Like Canada and the US, unemployment rates quickly skyrocketed to levels not seen in some countries' history. In others, including the UK and other countries in Europe, the labor market response was very different, with few workers laid off and most still working with their original employers, even if they worked from home. The differences in how labor markets are adjusted are a result of various factors. Factors like:

- the structure of the economy,
- the severity of the pandemic, and
- the intricate social contract between employers and their staff

played a crucial part in determining the effect of COVID-19 on the labor market.

How different countries took different policy choices to lessen the pandemic's economic effect and protect their workers is another critical factor.

Generally, most countries followed two principles: one, to emphasize income support for the workers who lost their jobs or livelihoods by providing them with stimulus packages, a better unemployment insurance plan, and other cash transfers; the other, to emphasize retention of jobs by subsidizing the wages, restricting layoffs and providing short-term compensation plans.

How successful the models were in the initial months of the crisis would offer note-worthy lessons to policymakers when dealing with future pandemics' immediate consequences.

Just as crucial for a full look is how countries using different policy models respond to the pandemic's subsequent waves, and eventually, how they fully restart their economies in a post-COVID world.

CHAPTER FOUR

POST PANDEMIC MONEY MANAGEMENT

Right-back from around November 2019, COVID-19 has been ravaging on in Asia, most especially in China, before spreading its tendrils in other parts of the world, straight to South and North America, down to Europe, and finally to Africa around March 2020.

The first few months were hard as everyone had to adjust to the new system of staying at home to curtail the spread rate as it was a global crisis and called a state of emergency and pandemic. The pandemic had its toll on everyone.

These ranged from the constant fear that existed in all when the mortality rate flared up with the health facilities stretched to its limits; schools were closed, religious centers, supermarkets, resorts, banks closed, and everything was on hold with a single notion in mind," to survive."

Apart from the emotional trauma everyone has been through, and another primary concern is your financial state. A lot of people lost their jobs during the pandemic. Others had their income slashed by the company they work for. Business owners went bankrupt, and for those full employment, there's this uncertainty in the air that the inevitable might happen, and they won't be an exemption. Perhaps you're one of the lots, and your financial situation has been a significant contention as to how possible it'll be for you to cope in this post-pandemic era. There are lots of things you can do to get back on your feet financially as regards steps and tips that'll help you manage your money in this post-pandemic period.

HOW TO MANAGE YOUR MONEY

1. First off-break down your finances by periodically checking and analyzing your finances concerning how things are and how things work presently.

The pandemic has affected our lives as well as the way we spend our money. It's essential to go through your accounts to check the loopholes effectively.

You should also check how much you've been able to save, your debts, and your rate of repayment. Strategizing the rate at which you spend is very important because it'll help you know when you're lapsing in your savings, the percentage you use for your emergency flow from your earnings, or if you're spending more on groceries.

For a period like this, you'll always have to make little adjustments to your budgets. Keeping track of your finances might be stressful. So, to avoid making mistakes, you can make use of budgeting apps on the play store. These apps will strategize your spending and schedule them in a single section that is easily accessible to you.

2. Reduce your debt rate, and to start with, you have to avoid new debt no matter small.

You might see flash sales during this period, and you may even be lured to get loans with small interest rates to get new gear, car, or machine.

Although, the things you get might have discount prices, one crucial thing you need to take note of is that debt will always be a liability, and even though the interest is at zero percent, which is mostly impossible, it's a loaned money, you'll have to pay back.

Although, the low-interest rate has its advantages, it can save you interest charges over the years, and perhaps you want to refinance your mortgage, you can go with a short-term loan. You can ask for low rates regarding your credit card, but that's only possible only if you have a good credit history.

You can also consider getting a balance transfer card with a low-interest rate. To save with your balance card, check the fees and plan to pay the balance before the period is over.

3. Cut out unnecessary expenses

You can start with eating at home. Virtually everyone knows that eating out costs more. The pandemic has made everyone stay home buddies, and we have almost no other choice than to eat in and spend once in a while to stock on groceries. For now, movements have been relaxed, and you might tend to eat out more, but it's advisable to eat at home more; this will help you reduce the way you spend.

Also, you will probably have to make a few reasonable cuts on your bills. You can save up the money realized on the excess bills and direct it to your emergency savings; just if anything happens, you won't be caught unawares.

You can start cutting in your billings with your streaming services. It doesn't necessarily mean you'll cut your spending. The primary thing is to rule out services you don't use quite often, and as regards your internet provider you can make inquiries about discounts and offers that'll be an advantage to you. The money realized from your meticulous budget can be saved and directed to clearing off debts.

4. Plan for the future.

Making periodical plans for your future might sound irrelevant as uncertainties creep on us before we realize them, but proper planning helps keep you on track. Although you can't predict what's to happen in the next few hours, still planning will help you get your stand amid eventualities.

Perhaps the second wave starts, and you have to work from home, or you are laid off friend work; what will you do then? Apart from the job you're running, what else can you do that'll fetch you extra cash just if you're unemployed? Having multiple sources of income is essential.

The online space has made it possible to work from home and still make money. You can take up freelancing as well as web development in your leisure. As important as your financial state is, your mental, physical and emotional health is also critical, and always make sure you avoid fake news and rumors.

It causes apprehension, anxiety, and fear. Always stay healthy by feeding well, exercising, taking enough rest, and staying safe by taking the necessary precautionary measures. When you get sick, you'll end up spending money, so it's essential to stay healthy.

The pandemic crept in on us unnoticed, leaving us with unforgettable effects. Many developed countries were hit so hard that their health care facility stretched out thin to the maximum, recording the highest fatality rate in the decade. As much as the pandemic affected us in the health sector, its effect on the financial aspect cannot be overemphasized.

Globally, the world market was hit with the rate of exchange dropping low. The international source of revenue each country generated also declined due to the imposed lockdown, shut airports, and closed ports, and truth, be told, to get to an excellent financial state, a proper financial master plan must be made.

It will help you get back to your financial position without really feeling the pandemic's effect on your finances. The most beautiful thing is that your financial status is not a determining factor in having a financial strategy.

You only have to go through a little processing that'll ensure you're financially stable. Below are outlined steps that'll help you in your money management in this post-pandemic era.

Step one: Know your financial status

The very first thing to do knows your financial position. You are getting to know the lapses and what needs to be addressed. Perhaps you have to make a cut on your budget as well as your savings.

Sometimes while assessing your finances, you get to know you have to increase the amount you save. As regards your investments, it's essential to know if you aren't on the losing end.

For your income, you have to note any changes in your income flow. For those who had their pay slashed due to the pandemic, you'll have to fit your budget to suit your current income flow.

Step two: Reevaluate your insurance policy

In case you have insurance, it's necessary to verify the coverage your insurance provides.

Often, a health insurance policy is the only policy most people sign up for. But now that we're in this post-pandemic era, it's advisable to ensure your family and loved ones are insured regardless. Getting a life insurance policy is a wise choice for yourself as well as your loved ones.

Step three: Have a budget and plan your expenses

Table your expenses and rate them in order of their importance. In case your income flow got reduced along with the cause of the pandemic, you will have to make few adjustments in your budget and plan your loan repayment if you were on loan during the pandemic period.

Step four: Create a flashpoint supply

I'm sure you're wondering what that is? A flashpoint supply is more like emergency money you've saved up. Many people had their flash point supply used up, but the fact that you have little or nothing left in your conserve doesn't mean you can't replenish it back step by step.

You can kick-start by keeping a 10th of your income. Just in case you come across a high-interest savings scheme, you can save up while you get more proceeds from the interest rate.

Step five: Get COVID-19 monetary aid

Perhaps the pandemic had a significant effect on your finances, and you can get monetary aid from financial institutions, government bureau, and non-governmental organizations. You can also get private loans with reduced interest rates.

No matter what, you can always prepare for the rainy day, and even though any eventuality might show up, you won't be caught unawares.

Step six: Take your time when it comes to shares

Many companies were hit hard during COVID-19 and ended up having their company shares reduced. A lot of people will see it as an opportunity to acquire shares.

Still, it's advisable to be well versed with investments before investing. Take your time, acquaint yourself with the situation on the ground. Don't be in haste to either buy or sell shares.

Most importantly, shun unnecessary extravagant spending and save up for flash point pool. Even though it looks like this is the best time to buy shares, it's most advisable to shun buying for a while because the pandemic has affected the country in such a way that it might take years to recover from.

You build your flash point pool, invest only in vital and essential services, shun extraneous spending, pay your debt and stay within your budget.

The pandemic is almost faint, but its imprint is still etched deep in our finances, and the next few months will be spanning through partial to total recovery.

So far, the lockdown had been draining the country financially, not to mention each individual. The more it extends, the more the financial state goes threads toward bankruptcy, and it all looks like a routine.

Crude oil prices hit rock bottom; the stock exchange is nothing to write home about. With the economy of nations facing challenges, we can say that the pandemic does greatly toll each individual's financial state, country, and the whole world.

Although, this is a post-pandemic period with relaxations on the extended lockdown with the government still putting preventive measures in place, even getting back to the way it was not easy, we all have to abide by a few rules and learn to live in this period.

To cope with the pandemic's effect on our financial position, we must learn how to manage our finances. As we all know, the second wave is imminent, and anything monetary is directed to our sustainability.

The financial state of each individual and each country is often in chaos. As such, everyone is always working around the clock to be in that sustainable position. Still, the arrival of COVID-19 only worsened things.

"Before the arrival of the pandemic coronavirus, the global economy was already experiencing turbulences. The situation has now been aggravated by demand, supply, and liquidity stocks; we have to reconsider our lifestyle expenses and essential expenses.

It is not a matter of maintenance of our standard of living but instead our living standard. We must rather maintain our living standard. Try to keep more cash in hand, considering you have a stable income, whatever loans are there, which generally bear a high rate of interest, try to repay those with existing sources of funds. Consecutively, try to pay at least 5 percent of outstanding home loans every year." (Vinayak Kulkarni.)

The most straightforward trick to make it through this post-pandemic era is to be financially stable. Make sure you build your flash point pool, invest only in vital and essential services, shun extraneous spending, pay your debt and stay within your budget.

CHAPTER FIVE

NEW INVESTMENT STRATEGIES AND HOW TO TAKE ADVANTAGE OF THEM

Investment is the process of devoting money to an endeavor with the expectation of receiving additional income. This extra income can be in the form of rent, interest, profit, or an increase in an asset's value. It is the process of building wealth and creating a life of financial abundance and freedom.

There are various reasons why people invest their money. The first of these reasons is to create wealth. Most people start trading their time, skill, knowledge, or expertise for money through their jobs. The restrictive characteristic is that their income is limited to a certain amount per month or per year.

Investing is a process that these people can use to make their money work for them. In other words, investment is a technique that allows investors to earn additional income on earned income. Investment vehicles like stocks, bonds, certificates of deposit, and so on allow people to create wealth over time.

Investment is also a smart way to prepare for the future. Young professionals and employees invest their earnings in preparation for when they are unable to work again. Investments allow them to gather funds together over time to create a reserve that they can live on after retirement.

There are several investment options available today. Some of them are:

Equity: this refers to ownership in a publicly-traded company. Publicly traded companies issue stock in a bid to raise capital to fund their activities. This provides private individuals with the opportunity to own a portion of the company.

When the company performs well, its stock appreciates, and the investor makes a profit. Many stock options also offer dividends so that investors get to enjoy an income payout option in addition to their investment.

Bonds: are similar to stocks in that they are used to raise capital to fund organizational activities, but unlike stocks, bonds can be offered by both companies and the government.

When an investor invests in bonds, they receive interests as regular payments until the maturity of their investment when they receive their full payment.

Preferred stocks: The primary difference between regular stock options and preferred stock is that preferred stock significantly lowers investors' risk.

Suppose an investor buys the preferred stock option from a company and the company goes bankrupt. In that case, the investor will be paid from the sales of company assets before any other investor is considered.

Also, while preferred stock options come with a fixed rate for dividend payments, regular stock options do not.

Mutual funds: these are aggregated funds collected from several investors by professional money managers. These experienced money managers invest the aggregated funds in various investment options like stocks, bonds, etc.

The advantage of mutual funds is that individuals who know little or nothing about money market instruments can invest successfully and grow their wealth.

There are several other investment options available today, and each comes with its risk levels. Usually, the higher the risk, the higher the potential earnings and vice versa. Other investment assets include real estate, cryptocurrency, precious metals, futures, derivatives, etc.

The COVID-19 pandemic has caused massive disruptions is in investing. In the early months of 2020, when the pandemic had just started ravaging the world, extensive damage was done to the global economy.

More than half of the world's population was forced to stay at home to curb the pandemic's spread, which caused virtually all economic activity to grind to a halt.

As a result of this occurrence, the global economy experienced a deep recession in the first half of the year. Several investment options were severely affected, and investors accrued massive losses.

For example, in March 2020, the S&P 500 fell in value by more than a third of its value. Several other assets experienced record low values as billions of investment dollars were flushed down the drain.

Later, towards the end of the year, the value of stocks and other related investment options skyrocketed. Many experts pegged the surge in the value of these investment assets on discovering COVID-19 vaccines and renewed the confidence of consumers.

The stock market also seemed to react positively to the election of President Joe Biden. The impact of the COVID-19 pandemic and the resulting recession was heavier on main street than it was on wall street.

Self-isolations, social distancing policies, lockdowns, and other safety measures to curb the virus's spread put an unparalleled strain on main street. Millions of businesses were shut down, and millions more were thrown into unemployment.

The many effects of the COVID-19 pandemic on wall street and main street have shown that it is easy for an economy to be extensively upturned in a short period. Knowing this, investors must better equip themselves to make wiser investment decisions.

Investors (old and new) must transform their perception of investment. It will help to guide against incurring massive losses in the case of another disruption to the economy.

In light of this, investors should fashion out new strategies. These new strategies should account for risk and provide cushions for such risk tailor-made for the post-covid world.

The need to think outside the box as investors at this point cannot be overemphasized because 2020 has shown that traditional investment strategies may not be as worthwhile moving forward.

The first thing to understand is that it may take some time for the global economy to fully recover from the damage that the COVID-19 pandemic has caused.

Even with the discovery of vaccines and the gradual return to normal,' there are still fears of a resurgence as countries completely re-open their borders.

In some developing countries, the virus is still ravaging. New strains of the virus have been detected in several developed countries, leading to another round of lockdowns.

Consumers are still skeptical about returning to pre-pandemic behavior, and many businesses are still yet to re-open. What this means is that investors must shift their focus to the long term. Experts project that real global economic growth and stability are only achievable in the long term.

So, moving forward, there are several factors investors should keep in mind. First, it is essential that understand that now is a wrong time to try to predict stock market movements. History has shown that the stock market tends to make roller-coaster movements in times of crisis.

It is evident from the stock market's movements in 2020 that things are still very volatile. Sharp movements can be great opportunities to make a lot of money, but they are also the same periods that investors incur massive losses. In the short run, it is wise to sit back and observe the market as it tries to find a steady rhythm before investing in the stock market.

Second, you need to diversify your portfolio. Diversification is crucial, especially during times of global economic uncertainty. The effect of diversification is that it helps you spread risk and reduces your chances of incurring unimaginable losses.

In other words, diversification helps you put your eggs in several baskets to minimize your losses if all the eggs in one basket got broken. If you are yet to, now is the time to diversify your investment portfolio to contain a wide range of options and investment asset classes.

When diversifying your investment portfolio, you must focus more on the quality of your investment options instead of focusing on the number of investment options. Quality investments will give you a more formidable stance in the event of disruptions.

In light of the current economic situation and the performance of the various sectors of the global industries, many investment options look promising, at least in the long run. These are companies that are expected to experience rapid growth in the post-covid era. Some of them have made low-carbon emission commitments in the long run by making their processes fossil-fuel-free. A similar investment option is mutual funds that have high Environmental, Social, and Governance ratings.

Companies that are conscious of their impact on the environment, society, and government are projected to be more sustainable, making them viable investment options for investors, especially in the long-term.

When comparing companies to invest in post covid, there are several key questions to ask yourself. One of them is how the company performed during the pandemic. How did the company respond to the radical change in the business scene? How did the lockdowns affect the company? Was the company able to implement a sustainable business model for the pandemic? Was the company able to maintain cash flow? What do the company balance sheets look like?

Finding the answers to these questions will help you ascertain precisely how valuable the company is, its resilience, and a viable investment option. Companies that were able to pull through the pandemic by responding swiftly to the changes it brought are more likely to thrive when the pandemic is finally over.

One of the investment sectors that performed wonderfully during the pandemic was the healthcare sector. The aggravated demand for quality healthcare in a time of crisis makes it a worthwhile investment option. Compared to the retail, tourism/hospitality industries, the healthcare sector flourished in 2020. The population is also aging, which means there will be a constant demand for quality healthcare. As such, growth potentials and earning prospects await investors in the healthcare sector.

Technology is another industry that proved itself during the pandemic. Technology allowed the world to keep on moving when the pandemic wanted it to stand still.

Children were able to learn from home; parents could work from home, and companies could function, all of which would have been impossible if the pandemic had occurred 30 years ago.

The increased adoption of technology and digitization to lower the pandemic's impact led to a rise in companies' value in the tech space. Zoom, for instance, gained more than 160% of its value and hit the $50 billion mark for the first time.

Technological innovations reduced the pandemic's impacts by no small measure, which is why companies in the tech industry are very viable investment options.

It goes without saying that you must ensure you do your due diligence before investing in any company or asset. A little research will help you make better investment decisions because it will open your eyes to things that you may have previously overlooked. While it is great to invest in assets that will attract a high R.O.I. in the short run, that should not be your focus in the short run.

With the current state of things, the best strategy is to invest strategically for the long term. That way, you will significantly reduce your risk and enjoy the benefits of compounding interest.

Compounding interest is one of the most potent aspects of investing. With a little strategy and some patience, compounding interest will help up grow your investment portfolio tremendously.

Another great strategy is to only invest in markets or assets that you understand well. When it comes to investing, it is essential to stick to what you know. If you encounter an investment 'opportunity' and find it impossible to understand its concepts and fundamental aspects, leave it.

If an investment option looks too good to be true, it most likely is. So, if you see an investment that promises to pay 58% R.O.I. every month, you should run away from it because it is almost certainly a scam.

You should also put conscious effort into blocking out all the noise. While it is essential to stay informed about the investment markets, you should be careful so that the flow of information does not become overwhelming and you begin to lose focus. Find creative ways to tune out all the noise and stay focused.

Like Warren Buffet once said, 'Be fearful when others are greedy and be greedy when others are fearful.' This means that you should be careful of what other people are doing in the investment market. Your investment decisions should not be based on 'that's what everyone is doing now.

While it can be comforting to be a part of the crowd when it comes to investment, but the truth is that the crowd is never on time. The crowd either arrives too early or too late. So, be independent in your investment positions and strategies.

Also, you should keep at the back of your mind that liquidity is essential in economically turbulent times. It is critical to invest strategically in very liquid assets. Investing in liquid assets will give you the upper hand in the event of any economic shocks like the pandemic brought.

Cash is king, so it is essential to have some money stashed out somewhere safe in case of unforeseen circumstances. In the event of a lockdown or any related measure, cash will come in handy to handle daily needs and operations. So, always have a backup hideaway somewhere.

An ideal way to store money for these scenarios would be a separate bank account to keep money in for emergencies. One other 'investment' strategy is to embrace financial prudence.

Take special care to cut off all unnecessary expenses and needless spending. Plan your economic activities ahead of time to eliminate all the little costs that add up to significant numbers over time.

Finally, investing can sometimes prove to be an overwhelming activity. It requires significant effort to research, observe and understand the market. It also involves a sense of discernment to map out profitable and sustainable strategies for investment.

If you are just starting, you might find that one or two things are a bit hard to understand. You can browse through the endless supply of resources on the Internet. Alternatively, you can speak to a professional investment adviser to get your questions answered.

CHAPTER SIX

ROLE OF THE ONLINE JOB MARKET AND HUMAN RESOURCES

A survey by the Bureau of Labor Statistics has shown that the rate of global unemployment has risen by 14.7%, beating the Great Depression in March 2009. This indicates that the worldwide pandemic (COVID-19) impact has a ripple effect globally, and the economy is finding it hard to find its balance.

In the United States of America,4 million fresh college graduates enter the labor market with no hope of getting a job anytime soon. This figure supports the research results in the United States that graduates who enter the Labor market during an economic recession will earn less than those who entered during a healthy economy.

This scary situation would have spelled doom or even be the end of the economies worldwide if not for technology's advent and development. C.E.Os shut down their companies due to the inability to manage the relentless punches the pandemic threw at them.

Many companies had to lay off their workers. Some reduced the wages of their workers by more than half of what they ought to earn typically. For workers still struggling with earnings that can barely take care of their daily and monthly expenses, reducing their earning would have driven many to frustration or even suicide. Both the employees and their employers had a taste of the bitter pill. The lockdown further worsened it all as people, especially those who feed from hand to mouth, could not go about their usual activities to put food on the table.

To move forward, online job markets and Human Resources (H.R.) will have to work hand in hand. The importance of these two cannot be overemphasized.

The economic effect of the global pandemic (Covid-19) includes the hastening of the digitalization processes. It is no longer debatable for companies to resort to digital platforms' immediate use to enable awareness and access to employment for their prospective employees.

Human Resource Management has a crucial role in assisting business and business organizations in finding their way through drastic changes they have to deal with, no thanks to the COVID-19 lockdown order.

Presently, the Covid-19 pandemic has caused demanding and endless conditions for human resource managers. Relating this to the dramatic changes throughout the globe due to the pandemic, organizations must learn to respond to these changes.

They must also manage the workforce in preparation for any other pandemic and tumultuous times in the future hit the world and disrupt the global system once again. They should adopt advanced technologies that are platform-based and come up with unprecedented business ideas and innovations.

H.R. professionals play facilitating and supporting role in business transformation, no doubt about that, but they also take responsibility to step up the employees by upgrading their skills and abilities.

Workers must learn new technologies, acquire new skills and skills and develop unique lifestyles alongside protecting the company's data and information. All these needs technological know-how to keep heads above water, sustain the output, improve efficiency and maximize materials.

This training should cover areas and aspects that have been subjected to the harsh implications of the COVID-19 pandemic. *These include areas such as:*

a. Public Relations: A very high percentage of companies and organizations have concerns about the gradual declining customer commitments and experience levels during the pandemic and lockdown.

It is mainly the case for customer-facing employees as well as companies and organizations that were forced to move third sales and products to online platforms. It has resulted in a whole new virtual community.

Changing the modus operandi from physical face-to-face interaction to honesty, trust, and value-based community and business organizations must speedily empower their workers to understand this recent work relationship and be actively involved and interact efficiently with customers.

b. Client's Experience: To establish and maintain a well-organized and coordinated client experience, giving the workers advanced digital technology skills is a crucial aspect to consider, adopting the use of digital tools, advanced analytics, for instance, which allows for sending messages to individuals personally and sales optimization.

Simultaneously, it increases the brand or company's presence on social media platforms can go a long way in enhancing good rapport and interaction with clients. Hence, improving client's experience rates.

c. Data security —Leveraging digital tools to enable productive new ways of working, Human Resource Managers in various companies need to pay prompt attention to ensure digital adoption.

They should also embrace and maximize technologies and processes that give room for employees to be more productive and efficient, especially when it comes to data security issues.

The most essential and fundamental requirement for effective offline working is possessing excellent internal processes for managing and maintaining data security. More than half of the companies examined plan to give rigidity to their data management procedures, given present data security's possible harm.

Human resource managers must make it a point of duty to train workers to be sensitive to online security threats and not forget to invest in the necessary cyber tools and skilled personnel to protect their offline and online workforce, clients, and organization.

In addition to the roles mentioned above of Human Resources, establishing a perfect online and offline environment for the employees to work is essential for its effective running. It is therefore vital to reassess the H.R. policies and practices during this Post COVID-19 period.

H.R. departments will play a significant role in developing new organizational priorities, aligning policies and practices, and bringing in related employee value supposition. Companies become actively involved in the business once again.

Areas that are expected to be covered include:

Workforce devising: There must be proper preparation and planning for staffing to handle the usual duties and special dues, for example, redeployment and essential and sensitive roles. Certain advantages must also be put in place to energize performance, rewards, and necessary facilities to improve overall workers relations.

Secondly, it is also essential to give space for employee flexibility. This can be achieved by institutionalizing offline working contracts that allow for individuals' limitations and provide them with work sequences that suit the unique circumstances that will not put them under any form of tension or apprehension.

It is also imperative for the H.R. to look into employee mobility. They must see to the ability of workers to move from one place to another conveniently.

To achieve this, there's a need to revise travel protocols, ensure and enforce compliance with travel regulations in the short-term, and modify executive travel policies as borders re-open for safe international travels.

Also, there's no moving forward any company that doesn't put the assurance, satisfaction, and wellbeing of her employees into consideration. It is necessary to define and implement policies that will account for employees' limitations and comfort levels, providing a clear and anxiety-free atmosphere for employees to express their concerns and worries.

This includes creating support groups and redesigning worker wellbeing programs to protect and promote mental health, wellness, and stability.

To add icing to the cake, it is worthy to say that a happy worker makes a pleased organization, and a hungry man is an angry man. The lockdown enforced due to the COVID-19 pandemic has done more than enough disadvantage to the employees. It is, therefore, necessary to enhance workers' motivation.

As organizations support and prepare their employees for a new course of action, priorities, and duties or assignments, they must focus on boosting their morale and efficiency through positive connection. It also means creating new means for workers to engage with each other, feel among, and inspired

A perfect example is creating opportunities for workers to work with each other and groups to interact with other workers, especially those within the same workspace while ensuring meaningful and impactful work.

In the same vein, there's an urgent call to review employee incentivization.

In an organization going through the post-COVID-19 season, organizations must understand and appreciate that productivity must be directly proportional to the employees' complete wellness. This is the only combination that will help employees flourish and be 100% relevant to the company.

Therefore, organizations need to take another good look at how they can best incentivize and motivate their workforce through practicable incentives and motivational mechanisms that be in monetary and non-monetary form.

These should be carefully rearranged in harmony with realistic performance expectations and designed with the utmost goal of ensuring employees flourish in this new work environment.

Having talked about the roles of Human Resources (H.R.), it is safe to say that the fisherman's importance is irrelevant if there are no fishes to catch. In simpler terms, it is saying that the H.R. cannot perform these roles if there are no employees to work.

In this technologically advanced globe we live in, almost everyone has access to the Internet and its associated facilities. A considerable percentage of the world, statistically speaking, more than 80% of the world's population, has an Android phone.

But very few of these individuals know the potency of the devices they carry around. Thanks to technology, it is straightforward to shop, send money, connect with people, and a lot of conveniences to go with the package. The ease of getting a job is not an exception. There had been so many testimonies of individuals inflating their bank account right there in their living room at the comfort of their sofas.

The latest trend is the use of online job markets like LinkedIn, Facebook, and Glassdoor. It is used by putting vital and marketable information about yourself as an employee and wait for the right employer to pick you up.

It is that easy. It has proven to be a very efficient tool in tackling post-COVID-19 terms and the workplace's movement online.

These channels have proven to be helpful in so many ways, which includes;

a. Boosting self-confidence: Being laid off from work can hit hard on people to a point where the realization shatters all hopes and every atom of self-confidence an individual can have. Some have committed suicide due to the heavy blow. These channels have served as a ray of hope of being employed and making money for people.

b. Bridging the Gap between prospective workers and employers: Job boards have fulfilled the need to create a link between unemployed individuals and real job opportunities. It has brought the employee and the employer closer by giving them a platform to meet and transact business. It has further reduced costs and risks on both ends as all these goodies come with the push of a few buttons on the device.

c. Technological awareness: There is nothing like a mismatch in skills between job seekers and employers. Both parties have a reason to embrace technology because the use of these job markets requires technological know-how. There is a need to learn and update oneself about the way around technology and fully maximize them to put themselves at a high advantage.

Maybe, just maybe, the pandemic had its sound effects because it has enhanced technologies' maximization.

However, it is imperative to note that effectively using these online job markets is an added advantage to prospective employees. Besides the ability to converse properly in English, specific skills need to be embraced to have the upper hand.

Getting a platform to get a job may be the easy part, but getting the job itself can be as tedious and competitive as it can be.

Recruiters use various technologically advanced communication tools like artificial intelligence (A.I.), employment outreach, and texting to reach out to job seekers.

Even the struggling companies are looking for ways to maneuver their way into virtual relevance to strengthen their teams. Hence, there is a need to keep up with this growing means of connecting to recruiters.

Communication skills are a critical aspect in online job markets as most employers look out for job seekers' abilities. The ability to express your thoughts in words fluently is a considerable advantage.

Build this skill by intentionally reducing the amounts of words used in a sentence. Be an addicted user of few words to express yourself. Also, try to intentionally look at people in the eye when talking to them. It helps boost confidence.

Also, always update yourself. Add value to yourself. Take courses offered online and carve a niche for yourself. Listen to the news and be conscious of the happenings in the world. Be actively involved in your community and take it upon yourself to solve problems. This gives you leverage and a professional outlook.

CHAPTER SEVEN

THE FUTURE OF REMOTE WORK

Remote work is the style of work that allows people to work outside of the conventional work environment. It is a practice that goes against many of the 'norms' of employment.

The traditional work concept is reporting at an office building sometime before nine in the morning, sitting at a desk to complete tasks/assignments, and leaving the office sometime after five in the evening.

The conventional style of work has prevailed for countless years, and while it has been able to bring the desired results, it makes no provisions for flexibility. There is only one way to work with this style, which is at your employer's location.

If you got a job in San Francisco, but you reside in New York, you would have to fly out to San Francisco. In most cases, you would have to relocate with your family, which means looking for a new house, a new school for the kids, new friends, and unique spots to hang out.

This hypothetical scenario shows how inflexible the traditional model of work can be. It also doesn't make any room for employees whose personalities are not inclined to cubicles and office politics.

Some employees are introverts, and as such, they are not great fans of office interactions. These kinds of employees are often overwhelmed by this amount of social contact, sometimes to the extent that it reduces their ability to perform optimally.

In the past, remote work referred to casual jobs handed down to unskilled/semi-skilled employees. Most of the remote jobs that existed then we're in customer service and rarely led to a full-time career.

In more recent times, remote work took the form of telecommuting. Employees who worked in sales and other related positions that required travel had to 'telecommute.'

These employees typically had to travel to meet clients and close deals as a part of their duties, but upon their return to the office, they would have to perform other behind-the-desk duties.

So, when they were in transit, usually in hotels in other cities, they would have to keep in contact with their home offices to ensure that they were in sync with their duties back home.

Today, remote work has evolved to the stage where remote workers run entire companies. People from any part of the world can work for companies from wherever. One great example of one such company is GitLab.

GitLab is an open-source software development company that has employees from as many as 65 countries. These employees are as many as 1200, and they all work remotely. GitLab had successfully operated this remote work model for several years, even before it became widespread.

When GitLab first adopted this remote work model, it had to provide all its recruits with an exhaustive handbook containing all the information and guidance they need to work remotely successfully.

The company also went out of its way to provide its employees with the tools and protocols that allowed them to interact and work together effectively, even when they lived several time zones apart.

Before the COVID-19 pandemic, several businesses already allowed some of their employees to work from home. Some were allowed to work from home a few days a week, while others came as part of a special arrangement.

At the time, companies were skeptical about the prospect of remote work because they feared that employees would slack off and not perform optimally if they were removed from the traditional office environment.

They believed that direct (physical) supervision and face-to-face interaction with colleagues were prerequisites for optimal performance.

In the wake of the pandemic, when people were forced to remain at home due to isolation, social distancing policies, and lockdowns, companies had to adapt quickly to prevent irreparable damage to their businesses. Remote work became the only way out for companies to continue running.

Last year (2020), when the lockdown came into effect, the percentage of remote workers climbed sharply from only 3.4% in February to 42% in April. It was an extraordinary surge that the remote work scene had never experienced before. Employees began to realize that they can perform the same tasks they did in the office within their homes' comfort.

Zoom, a teleconferencing platform, experienced an incredible influx of users as Zoom meetings became the new normal. Teleconferencing and other related technological innovations have made it possible for employees to have real-time 'face-to-face' communication regardless of where they are as long as an internet connection is available.

The sharp increase in the proportion of millennials in the workforce today is another factor that has greatly influenced the widespread of remote work. This new set of employees are bent on having the freedom to live their own lives outside their daily jobs. Therefore, they are unwilling to take on any positions that will restrict them to a physical location.

Millennials and Gen-Z employees want to have good high paying jobs, but they also want to have their own lives. In other words, unlike the older generation, these workers want to work to live, not live to work. Their mindset and demands are rapidly reshaping the way we work and pushing the widespread adoption of remote work.

Remote work, however, doesn't have a fixed form. When you think of remote work, the image that immediately comes to mind is that of an employee sitting at a table in a make-shift home office while the kids are up to some kind of mischief in the next room, but this is not necessarily the truth of remote work.

While working from home is the most prevalent form of remote work, there are several other creative ways people work from outside of their offices. Yes, a home office is probably the most convenient way to go about it. Different methods include the hybrid form of remote work and work and travel arrangements.

The hybrid form of remote work is quite common today. Employees are allowed to work from home or at co-working facilities in the same area as their company. This arrangement only lasts for some days of the week. On these days, they can perform tasks that require intense concentration and solitude. On other days of the week or a day of the week, they report to their employer's location to perform other tasks that require one-on-one interaction with colleagues and superiors. This arrangement allows for a higher level of flexibility than the traditional work model, and it is already being implemented by several employers today.

Another variation of the remote work model is the work and travel option. Today, many people take the opportunity to travel and explore the world (or some parts of it) and work simultaneously. This set of remote workers can choose to either travel solo or as a group. Whichever option they choose, it will require the consent of their employers.

In this case, the remote worker and his/her employer will have specific terms that they will agree to. These terms will include Key Performance Indicators that define the tasks/duties that the employee will be required to perform and other specific details.

After their employers' permission, work, and travel, remote workers can create a personal schedule that allows them to enjoy their trips while also completing their employers' tasks.

They typically look for coffee shops, co-working spaces, and other places with fast internet connectivity to work for the hours they set aside for work. When they don't have to work at different periods, they can fully immerse themselves in the tourist lifestyle and take whatever environment they find themselves in.

With the discovery of vaccines for the coronavirus, things are beginning to seem like they will return to normal. The thing, however, is that people may not want to return to the previous model of work.

The short exposure to remote workability across industries has shown that remote work is a sustainable one with little effort on the employees' and employers' sides.

Remote work is forecasted to continue well after things return to normal as many companies and employees have seen firsthand the many benefits that accrue. The number of co-working spaces exploded in 2020 and is expected to continue as more businesses provide remote work options for their employees.

Big names like We Work have responded to increased demand by providing practical and comfortable co-working spaces across the country. These co-working spaces are built with the comfort and convenience of remote workers in mind.

Amenities like 4G WIFI, air condition, coffee/tea rooms, food courts, and even soundproof rooms are expected to flood the co-working space scene in the nearest future.

In the same vein, remote work arrangements that came as an adaptation to the safety policies to slow the spread of the COVID-19 pandemic will become permanent. A Gartner C.F.O. survey reported that 74% of companies already have plans to make remote arrangements permanent.

Big companies like Twitter and Facebook have already communicated to most of their staff who had to shift to working remotely to continue indefinitely even after the pandemic ends.

Companies that will not completely shift to a fully remote working model will most likely adopt a hybrid form of the remote work model. Here employees will be allowed to work remotely for some days of the week to complete individual tasks or other duties they can accomplish solitarily.

Then on a day (or two days) of the week, they will be required to report to their employers' location for meetings, brainstorming sessions, or other activities that require collaboration and physical interaction.

Similarly, the work environment post-covid is forecasted to be more equitable. In the past, workers who opted to work remotely had to let go of certain benefits or allowances.

It was the case because most employers did not believe employees can be as productive when working outside the office environment. These employees had to trade specific incentives for the freedom of remote work.

Moving on from the present state of things, predictions show that reverse will be the case moving forward. Most companies will now provide incentives for workers who choose to work remotely.

Employers will begin to offer specific allowances, tools, and other incentives to employees who opt to continue working remotely.

Employers' focus will shift from all the peripheral things like employee dress code and sociability to other things that move the needle, like the results that each employee can deliver.

Introverted employees who find constant social interaction overwhelming will now perform at their peak because remote work provides the optimal environment for them to work.

In the same vein, the focus on results will allow for the trend of condensed weeks to flourish. A condensed week is a phenomenon that occurs when employees choose to work longer hours for fewer days of the week to deliver the same results they are required to provide for the week.

For example, if a graphic designer is supposed to work 9 am-5 pm Monday through Friday and deliver 20 infographics, he/she can decide to work 8 am-6 pm from Monday to Thursday, produce all 20 infographics and begin the weekend on Thursday evening.

The condensed week is a trend that is rapidly growing among the younger generation of employees who prefer to work longer hours to achieve a shorter workweek. They can then invest the extra free time in personal activities like traveling or even freelancing.

Similarly, the gigging or freelancing industry is expected to grow with the proliferation of remote work arrangements. When employees are allowed to perform company tasks on their terms, they can create schedules for themselves.

With this schedule, they can dedicate specific hours for completing company tasks while they spend the rest of their time freelancing on the side. It is projected that employees will begin to turn down traditional jobs even when the pay is high and prefer to take on remote positions with lower income because of the freedom and flexibility that these positions will avail them of.

Freedom to determine their schedule and spend more time on personal exploits outweighs the benefits of higher pay. The future of remote work also entails a portends a sharp reduction in the need for office space. As more and more employees decide to work remotely, companies will experience a lesser need for office space.

Cubicles and other traditional work model requirements will phase out gradually, and companies will move into smaller, more practical buildings.

Companies like R.E.I. have already begun the move as they announced the sale of their un-used 8-acre campus in Bellevue, Washington. The company's C.E.O., Eric Arts, explained that the company would "lean into remote working as an engrained, supported, and normalized model" for employees.

R.E.I. is only one of the many companies whose eyes have opened to the benefits of embracing remote work models as it would reduce office space. Operating a smaller office space will go a long way to reduce the various costs that large office buildings attract.

As employees begin to work from home and companies function out of smaller spaces, most of the world's busiest cities will transform into greener, quieter, and more livable environments. Many of these big cities are so crowded and tedious to live in because opportunities are most available there.

As remote work becomes more widespread, employees will move away from busy cities and relocate into small towns. Since they can work from anywhere, they are not physically 'tied' to any location, and so they will look for places that align more with their personalities.

As a result, cities will become less dense; there will be less traffic, lower emissions, and living costs will fall to more reasonable levels.

Small towns on the receiving end of this migration will enjoy increased tax dollars and general economic prosperity. Many smaller cities like Pagosa Springs and Salida have started providing incentives and an attractive environment to attract remote workers who leave the busier larger cities.

Studies have shown that when people leave the smaller cities searching for higher-paying jobs in the cities, they never stop missing 'home.' They usually still find it hard to form the kind of bond they have with their hometowns with the big cities.

With the proliferation of remote work, it becomes possible for these workers to return to their hometowns where they can feel at home and invest in such places while performing at their highest levels of productivity.

Another trend worth mentioning is the increasing number of countries that are offering remote work visas. Countries like Estonia, Dubai, and Barbados have since last year started offering professionals from across the world visas that allow them to live and work remotely in their countries.

The remote work visas would enable these professionals to stay for up to a year and even let them file for a visa extension if they meet some specific minimum income requirements.

With remote work visas, professionals will be able to migrate to these countries and make good money while exploring their new environment. Some professionals have already taken advantage of this development and have migrated with their families. Host countries typically boast of flexible visa options, extensive and affordable 4Glte internet coverage, reasonably priced accommodation options, comprehensive health care coverage, and excellent school options for those traveling with their kids.

Finally, it is projected that there will be a surge in platforms' size and efficiency that facilitate remote hiring, payroll services for remote workers, and other related bodies. Before now, companies used to face severe issues with hiring remote staff, the legal tenets that apply to recruiting remote staff, and payroll solutions for the remuneration of remote workers.

These issues will soon evaporate with companies and agencies' proliferation dedicated to providing employers with these exact solutions. Platforms like Boundless, Xolo, Panther, Deel, Remote team, and so on specialize in the various steps and procedures pertinent to remote hiring, payroll, and legal requirements.

Remote work has come to stay. The COVID-19 pandemic has no doubt accelerated the adoption of the remote work model across industries. As a result of this exposure, most companies and their employees will stick to the remote work model to enjoy its benefits.

CHAPTER EIGHT

HOW TO PREPARE FOR VIRTUAL INTERVIEWS

The coronavirus has undoubtedly changed the face of business since it became a global pandemic in the early months of 2020. The enforcement of social distancing measures, self-isolation, and country-wide lockdowns have led to radical transformations in the way companies ran their businesses.

Pandemic or not, some business processes still have to occur because they are vital to any organization's healthy functioning. One of such processes is the recruitment process. Even as safety policies are in effect, companies worldwide still recruit suitable candidates to fill vacant positions.

Remote workers can fill several vacant positions that are open in these companies. In other words, companies can hire qualified professionals from any location to fill vacant positions as long as they meet the requirements and successfully pass the recruitment process.

In a bid to keep everyone safe and curb the spread of the virus, companies must adhere strictly to all the safety guidelines stipulated by the government and its agencies. As a result, employers cannot conduct face-to-face interviews like they used to do before the pandemic.

Companies now conduct virtual interviews. Unlike traditional face-to-face interviews, virtual interviews rely on video conferencing technology and, as such, do not require any form of physical contact between employers and applicants.

Employers can successfully interview candidates from anywhere, either over the phone (on a voice call) or using video conferencing technology such that they can see and hear each other in real-time.

Although virtual interviews share many similarities with traditional interviews, virtual interviews require extra care and special preparation.

In other words, preparing for a virtual interview is quite similar to preparing for a traditional interview. You will, however, have to take extra precautions and make special arrangements for the peculiar features of a virtual interview.

Like with a traditional interview, the first step to preparing for a virtual interview is to read through the job description carefully. The job description is the information that the employer provides concerning the job. It will typically contain details like the required qualification, experience, personal qualities, and other criteria the employer is looking for in the ideal candidate.

The information provided in the job description should serve as a guide for you. From the job description, you will understand the employer's needs and even some questions that he/she is likely to ask during the interview.

The job description will contain enough information to know if you are qualified for the position and ascertain precisely why you are interested in the job.

You should discern if the qualities the employer requires are those you possess and if the job's values align with your values. It would be best to be convinced that you are the perfect fit for the position and demonstrate this to the employer.

Once you have identified some reasons why you are interested in the position and are convinced that you are a perfect fit for the job, it's time for you to do some digging.

You have to research the company you are applying to. There are countless benefits of doing some digging concerning the company. For starters, it will give you a deeper understanding of what you are getting yourself into.

You will learn about its core values, how long it has been in existence, its position in the industry, and other information that will give you an edge during the interview. When you are doing your digging, you will need to find out as much as possible about the product or service that the company offers.

A company's product or service is usually at the center of its operations, so knowing a thing or two about it will help you understand how you will fit into the larger picture. Being able to demonstrate this knowledge is a sure way to stand out from the crowd of applicants.

You should also extend your research to investigate the details of the role you are applying to fill. Go the extra mile to learn about every (or almost every) responsibility of filling the role. Understand exactly what you will be required to do and the day-to-day demands of the position.

Researching the role will help you confirm if you are indeed a perfect fit or otherwise. It will also help you formulate thoughtful and meaningful questions to ask during the interview.

One of such questions is 'What are typical daily routines that the role entails? Who are the colleagues that you may need to collaborate with if give the job? Asking these kinds of questions will help you make a lasting impression in the mind of the interviewer. He or She will perceive you to be very serious and genuinely interested in the position, and this can make all the difference.

Your research should touch on the culture of the company. You should aim to find out how things are run where you hope to work. Seek out answers to questions like- what is different about the environment?

What provisions do they make for sick employees? Will you get a vacation? What software or computer application do they use? Digging deep on the Internet, especially if the company has a blog on their website, will help you answer these questions. You can also prepare questions ahead of the interview if there are certain areas that you do not fully understand.

You can then proceed to prepare answers to common interview questions. The truth is that you may not be able to predict all the questions that you will be asked but preparing solutions for the most common ones will put you in a better position to ace your interview.

Below is a compilation of 25 common interview questions:

1. Why did you leave your previous job?
2. What interests you about this position?
3. What makes you different from all other applicants?
4. Why do you want to work with us?
5. Tell us about yourself?
6. What is your passion?
7. Where do you see yourself in the next, say, five years?

8. Why should we hire you?

9. What are your salary expectations?

10. Have you ever failed before? How did you handle it?

11. How do you handle the pressures of work?

12. What are your personal goals?

13. What can you bring to this company?

14. What are your greatest strengths?

15. What are your most significant weaknesses?

16. Can you walk us through your resume?

17. Who are our competitors?

18. Are you willing to travel?

19. What are the things you plan to accomplish in the first 30 days of this job?

20. Describe a time you got angry at work.

21. Describe a time you disagreed with a superior.

22. Would you ever lie for this company?

23. Describe your ideal work environment.

24. Do you consider yourself a leader?

25. What the name of the last book you read?

These are only a few common interview questions that you can practice answering as you prepare for your virtual interview. While there are many more, these will give you some insight into the type of questions that you should expect during the interview.

Answering these questions requires skill and poise. You are allowed to take a moment to gather your thoughts before you answer. Don't take the whole of five minutes to gather your thoughts. That will be awkward, and you don't want that in your interview. You can use the STAR formula to provide robust answers to these questions.

The STAR formula is convenient when you are asked to answer a behavioral question. Behavioral questions are those that an interviewer uses to gauge what your response will be in specific scenarios.

The purpose of behavioral questions is to give the interviewer a clear picture of what your response will be to various work scenarios. They are used to assess the various qualities you possess and how you can apply these qualities in real-life work situations.

For example, suppose an interviewer asks you to describe a time when you disagreed with a superior. In that case, he/she wants to gauge how you will *behave* if you disagreed with a superior should they hire you. It is where the STAR formula will help you make the best impression.

STAR is short for Situation, Task, Action, and Result. These four elements will help you prepare powerful answers to behavioral questions by narrating an experience in a way that will convince the interviewer that you are a perfect fit for the role.

The first element is the situation. It will be the introductory part of your narrative. It is where you will provide the interviewer with information on the context of the events that occurred. Here, you will give just enough details that the interviewer can paint a mental picture of the situation.

However, it would be best if you were careful not to overdo it. Ensure you only provide useful information and don't chip in trivial details irrelevant to the narrative.

The second element you should include in your response is the task. Here, you should inform the interviewer of the task that you had to perform. In unambiguous terms, narrate the goals that you had to attain in the given situation. Like with the situation element, you should be as brief as possible.

Be careful not to include any extraneous information; get straight to the point. The next element is the action. It is where you go into the details of the process you followed to complete the task you were faced with.

The action part of your answer is arguably the most important, so you are allowed to be as descriptive as possible. Walk the interviewer through the exact steps you took that helped you to achieve the results that were required of you.

Here you might be tempted to narrate how your team or your group managed the situation, but that's not really what the interviewer wants to hear. The interviewer is trying to hire you, not your team. So, feel free to use the word 'I' as much as you need to.

Say 'I did....', 'I spoke to...', 'I set up.......' The information you provide here will paint a picture that will help the interviewer decide whether or not you are the best fit for the role.

The final element is the Result. It is also as important as the action element because the interviewer is also interested in the results you achieved. You should, however, try to spend less time here than you spent narrating the actions you performed. Go straight into describing the outcomes of your efforts and how you were able to learn from them.

It would help if you could get a friend or relative to help with a mock interview to answer these common interview questions with the STAR formula. Enough practice will help you gain confidence and fluency with answering the questions.

Next is to pick a location for your virtual interview. Because you will not be going to your employer's physical location for the interview, you are in control of the venue, and you should use it to your advantage.

A quiet area of your home will be a very great option. Pick a location that is devoid of distractions where the interviewer will be able to focus on you. It could be in a dedicated home office, your bedroom, or even on the kitchen counter as long as there will be no background noise and nobody will move around.

If you have children or share your space with housemates, you will have to politely request that you need some quiet time during your interview. If you have pets, you might have to place them in a cordoned-off area or have the friendly neighbor look after them for a bit.

Once you have the location settled, the next thing is to pick your attire for the interview. Virtual interviews are no different from traditional interviews when it comes to dressing. It would be best if you put on a formal or, in some cases, semi-formal attire.

A simple ironed button-down shirt will suffice whether you are a man or a woman. A nice pair of pant trousers will also work but keep in mind that the interviewer is not likely to notice what you are wearing below the waist.

Your face will focus on attention, so apply minimal make-up, ensure that your hair is not covering your face and that you aren't wearing any distracting accessories.

The next thing is to test your technology to ensure that everything is in order. Virtual interviews rely on video (or voice) technology, so you need to make sure that your microphone and webcam are working correctly.

You should also make sure you have the latest version of the software platform on which the interview is scheduled to hold.

Download the software and set it up at least a day before the interview. Test if your microphone and camera work correctly with the software and practice speaking to the camera to get familiar with it.

An excellent way to go set up is to place your laptop on a table or countertop in front of you. That way, your face appears in the center of the screen. Make sure you are not too far or too close from the screen so that the interviewer can see your face. A handy tip ensures that there's not too much space above or below your face on the screen.

Thirty minutes to the interview, log in to the video conferencing software, do a final check to make sure you haven't missed anything, and patiently wait for the interview to begin. When the interview commences, you should smile politely and maybe even wave at the interviewer as a show of courtesy.

It would be best if you also considered sending a follow-up email within 24 hours of the interview to show continued interest in the role. A follow up email thanking the interviewer for their time will go a long way to leave a lasting good impression. You can also include in the email that you are willing to provide any other information the employer may require.

Good luck!

CHAPTER NINE

ONLINE RESOURCES AND SYSTEM OF SUPPORT

ONLINE RESOURCES AND SYSTEM OF SUPPORT

Whether remote or not, the beginning or any career is getting a job on hand first, traditionally looking for a job often evokes nervousness and anxiety. In more recent times, Job seekers hire job recruitment agencies or wake up to the day's newspapers to rummage through classified ads to find vacancies that they qualify for.

Today, however, things are a little different. As the backbone of modern remote jobs, the Internet has a system of application that simplifies the job search process and provides real-time feedback to you – as a job seeker.

WHERE TO LOOK FOR A JOB

Depending on the time of job you are looking for, there are incredible job search resources online. Some of them end their service by providing a classified list of available openings, the requirements, and information on how to apply. Others stay in between managing your relationship with your employers. In contrast, others have a more concrete system of support.

Company Websites

The most direct means of seeking a job online is to visit company websites. But this is more useful when you have a clear idea of who you want to work for and are armed with unique expertise. Otherwise, your efforts can be ineffective and rather tiresome.

Companies and organizations usually leave a page open that displays available job openings, requirements, and information on applying for them. It would be best if you started with making a list of websites you are interested in.

Job Boards

There are hundreds, probably thousands of websites that have built platforms to connect employers and talented job seekers. Most of them are industry-specific, catering to the need of a particular job type.

They often provide a listing of available jobs, requirements, and methods of application. Some of the more popular job boards are Indeed.com, Monster.com, FlexJobs.com, Glassdoor.com, Scouted.com, Justremote.com, etc.

Freelancing Platforms

If you are a flexibility fanatic and don't like being tied down to a specific company, you can work based on projects and milestones – mostly on your terms. Freelancing websites brings clients (which could be either individuals or organizations) with specific assignments and tasks.

They also act as escrow to facilitate a trusted transaction where both parties are catered to. Upwork.com, Fiverr.com, Freelancer.com are popular freelancing platforms where you can find hundreds of listings in your field of expertise to work on projects on a freelance basis.

UTILIZING LINKEDIN, GLASSDOOR, E.T.C.

While there are many job search platforms and resources on the Internet, two giants stand out. They are particularly impressive because of their widespread influence, catering to millions of professionals and companies.

Each with a unique and modern approach to finding employment for job seekers, but like every tool, the effectiveness lies in the way you go about using it. Let's take a brief look at how to best use Glassdoor as a job search tool.

Glassdoor and LinkedIn provide a listing of millions of available jobs for the benefit of job seekers. The platforms bring an element of transparency to the job-seeking process, so you build relationships and form a vivid idea of what you are getting yourself into.

In the past, information about companies, especially in detail were rare to find, even on the Internet. The little known is often what the company itself makes available – which often is not never really sufficient to make an educated decision about working for them but cannot be relied on to represent the truth.

On the one hand, Glassdoor has created an excellent window into most companies today, with the information provided by employees themselves. The system takes many data from multiple employees in different organizations, analyzes, authenticates, and organizes them into a structured database for future job seekers.

The platform runs on a system of ratings and reviews, making it easy to make conclusions at a glance. You are better able to match vacancies with your goals and can take control of your work-life and your career in general from the very beginning

LinkedIn is a more social job search tool that focuses more on making a network of people with mutual benefits to advance your careers. With a network of trusted allies, it becomes easy to find available opportunities that are often not open to the public. You can also connect with past workers and employers who can stand as guarantors and referees in future endeavors.

The next few paragraphs are dedicated to making the best use of Glassdoor and LinkedIn as a job-seeking tools.

Create a Profile

To take advantage of these platforms, you have to start with creating a profile. First, you have to visit their websites, glassdoor.com and linkedin.com, respectively. After you find their "sign up" icon, you will be requested to create a profile.

In creating your profile, you will need to provide your name, resume/CV, and a short introduction. After these, you will be required to choose your professional skills, expertise, experience, and contact information from a list.

See the profiles as an opportunity to display your expertise and talents, as the profile is the first thing recruiters see when they are looking for talents from the platforms.

Find Job Openings

You don't have to wait until you are contacted by a recruiter either. Both LinkedIn and Glassdoor have a perfect search engine that helps you sift through available jobs. You can personalize the tool s it brings you jobs based on preferred conditions like the location, distance, job type, average salary, and so on.

Also, Glassdoor has an impressive tool that helps you create job alerts. This tool brings you daily job openings to your inbox based on your preferred conditions. Hence, you don't have to stalk job openings every hour of your day continually.

Build Relationships

It is particular to LinkedIn and can take a bit of time. Even more, the Result is rarely immediate, but building relationships can bear tremendous benefits for your job opportunities. LinkedIn helps its users connect and build a network. The more intimate the relationship you build with the relevant people, the higher stronger your network is. Strong recommendations and endorsement from your network significantly increase your chances of gaining employment becomes.

Join Professional Groups

Another essential feature you need to use is LinkedIn groups. There are already thousands of professional groups where your peers hang out. Being an active member of such a group will give you an edge when an opportunity comes knocking.

You get access to firsthand information about seminars, resources, job openings, etc. But it is equally important to take the time to research the groups. Chances are, there is more than one group available for your profession or niche. Some are more active and more inclusive than others.

Check out Company Review, Salary, and Benefits.

Over time, you will start getting job opportunities that pique your interest. You can now truly benefit from your peers by going through ratings and reviews to get a good sense of the company or organization.

You also get a pretty good idea of how much a company pays for your position. You will even know how it corresponds to your worth. It is possible with Glassdoor's "Know Your Worth" that briefly outlines how much you should be making.

Insights on other benefits are often provided as well, especially for well-established companies.

Check out Interview Questions

Once you find a job that interests you, you can go further along and check out interview questions available on the platform. Previous interview questions are often left on Glassdoor by employees ahead of you, together with difficulty stats and interview processes. All these will get you prepared mentally.

Apply

The final phase of your job-seeking process on these platforms is to apply for said jobs. Even though each of the two platforms allows direct application for employment, recruiters rarely use the feature. Instead, you are required to continue the application on the employer's website. Here, you will be given information on how to proceed. Often you will be required to submit your CV/Resume plus a cover letter, together with your contact information.

ONLINE EXAMINATIONS AND CERTIFICATIONS

As remote work gains popularity among employers, recruiters use a series of details to narrow down their search for qualified candidates. One effective way they do so is to filter using online examination and certifications.

As a job seeker, it becomes vital to stay up-to-date with trusted certifications that verify your expertise. It is essential for soft skills that aren't learned in an organized school setting. Specialized roles also require advanced certification that can easily be obtained from the Internet.

Like other remote work aspects, you can now quickly obtain certifications from trusted and respected online institutions. Taking examinations and certifications offers much flexibility. Here is how you use online resources to obtain certifications.

Identify the Certifications You Need

Your goal would determine your route. Getting a good idea of what recruiters use in shortlisting applicants would gear you towards the right path. It is quickly done by going through job listings. Recruiters often leave requirements in their job listings.

Another way is to check out profiles of successful individuals who work in a similar role to what you are looking for. Often, a certification pattern would emerge, and you can make go on to find a way to get your certification online.

Find a Good Certification Platform Online

You will be surprised by the number of certifications available for most fields. With scores of online institutions offering them at varying conditions and prices. Even physical institutions like Harvard and Princeton offer tons of online certifications that do not require you to step out of your house.

The next step is to figure out which platform offers the best certification under the best prices for you. Some popular websites where you can obtain certificates include Lynda.com, Coursera.com, Udemy.com, etc.

Taking Online Examinations

Before you are granted the certification, you are often required to take a test or an examination to assess your proficiency. Hence, the need for adequate preparation.

First, you go through the outlines to see what see subjects you will be tested on. In preparation for the test, you can consult provided resources. You are taking practice tests when available bear tremendous results also. Not only would you confirm your ability, but you will also be exposed to the examiners' test style.

Once you are confident of your ability to pass the test, you have to find a calm, quiet spot. If you can't get that in your home, you can use a local library. Don't forget to tune your time-management skills as well.

To become a high-value employee or employment candidate, you should always keep up with new certifications available and update your online profiles accordingly.

NEW GENERATION CV/ RESUME

Post coronavirus pandemic and the new age of remote employment have recruiters looking for different skills and abilities. For example, employers pay special attention to applicants with little work experience. It is tedious and time-consuming to induct new employees into adequate remote working conditions.

It makes it necessary for you to review your CV/resume to ensure that it states your skills and experience that edges you above other applicants. If you have remote work experience, you should make it as visible as possible for employers to see at a glance. It includes having it in your resume summary, under your work experience, etc.

When describing your skills, you should include all the software and resources you are familiar with that facilitate remote work, such as communication, sharing, and assessments.

Digital media is here to stay, and your CV/resume and certifications have to be converted to formats congruent to this form. Most employers require you to send them your resume via email nowadays. Hence, the need to have your documents available in pdf format, the most requested digital format. Although sometimes, you can be required to leave your documents in doc. Format.

You should pay attention to format details when applying for jobs online. Else, your application can quickly be disqualified without consideration.

SUMMARY

In December 2019, the novel coronavirus was first reported in Wuhan, a Chinese city. The virus was said to be highly contagious and was a severe cause for concern.

By March 2020, the virus had spread from the Chinese city of Wuhan to almost every corner of the planet, which informed the World Health Organization (WHO) 's decision to tag it as a global pandemic.

In the weeks that followed, every country in the world put several measures and policies to curb the spread of the virus. Self-isolation was mandated for people who may have been exposed to the virus.

Social distancing measures were enforced to prevent human-to-human transmission of the virus by contact, infected persons were quarantined, and lockdowns were imposed.

As a result of all of these measures, the once rapidly moving world was stopped in its tracks. Countries closed their borders to shut off international travelers, businesses had to shut their doors, schools asked pupils/students to stay back at home, and the world came to a standstill.

It was a strange experience, something straight out of a movie. A new normal emerged as people began to adapt to the radical changes in their lifestyle. Every sector or industry had to either adapt or be obliterated by the global pandemic's unforgiving reality.

Schools soon realized that what was to be a short break was going to become a very long one indeed. They had to fashion out ways on how to teach their pupils and students from their homes. The students and pupils also had to adjust to the new learning style and interaction with their colleagues.

Millions of employees lost their jobs as businesses struggled to cope with the pandemic's harsh economic reality. The employees who still had jobs had to adapt to the new normal of working from home where possible.

Teleconferencing and other related technological innovations were at the fore of this adaptation as they facilitated the exchange of information between employers and employees. Platforms like Zoom were at the forefront of this revolution, and remote work became widespread worldwide.

Small businesses were severely impacted by the pandemic and the resulting safety measures. Millions of businesses closed down permanently as customer orders dropped to zero.

Others who were able to weather the storm had to let go of several staff to compensate for revenue loss. Several observers opined that main street was probably the most severely affected victim of the pandemic.

Multi-National corporations were also gravely hit by the harsh reality of the pandemic and the resulting changes. Massive disruptions in the global demand chain and supply network resulted in heavy losses for many of these companies. Many of these large corporations had to scale down their operations significantly and even retrenched thousands of their staff.

The country's healthcare system was stretched to its extreme limits by the rapidly increasing number of infection cases. Hospitals and other healthcare facilities were full to the very brim, and a scarcity of personal protective equipment soon followed.

The demand for sanitary items like alcohol-based hand sanitizers, latex gloves, nose masks, face shields, and so on skyrocketed as people scrambled to keep themselves safe from the virus.

In no small measure, the government tried to cushion the many adverse effects of the pandemic on the country. Financial aid totaling trillions of dollars was distributed to individuals and businesses.

It was in a bid to alleviate the symptoms of the ensuring job crisis. These came in the form of stimulus checks, social security payments, interest-free loans, and other programs that are still being implemented today.

Now, with the discovery of COVID-19 vaccines and other related developments, things are gradually beginning to look up. People have started moving forward with their lives with a positive mindset, even in the face of uncertainty. Consumer confidence is slowly returning, and businesses are re-opening.

It is improbable that things will ever return to the way they were before the pandemic. The past year has exposed just how fragile we truly are as a people, and we must learn from that experience so that we march into the next phase wiser. We must not only live. Differently, we must also strategize because the variables have changed.

Remote work, for instance, that many employers frown upon, became the only work model that succeeded during the pandemic. The number of remote positions increased exponentially in 2020, and from all indications, it appears that remote work is here to stay. Many companies have decided to allow their staff to retain the current arrangements even after the pandemic has disappeared.

We also have to approach money and personal finance from a different angle. The events that followed the pandemic have made it crystal clear that individuals, businesses, and even nations have to take a different approach towards money.

As individuals, now more than ever, it is essential to plan out personal finance activities and objectives. New approaches to spending and investing must be mapped out to avoid a repeat of the events of 2020. Everyone must now take personal finance and financial literacy as a critical aspect of life.

For those who have lost their jobs to the pandemic, online platforms and resources are vital to finding employment. Job seekers must learn how to leverage these platforms in their job search because they now play a more dominant role in the recruitment process in the post-covid era.

Another part of the recruitment process that has had to evolve because of the pandemic is the interview part. Safety measures have made it impossible to hold on-site physical interviews, so companies resort to conducting virtual interviews.

Virtual interviews, although similar to traditional on-site interviews, also has their peculiarities. Job seekers must know to effectively prepare for virtual interviews to impress employers and land high-paying jobs.

There is no doubt that the COVID-19 has changed the world. We can already see many of the changes that it has brought, and many will still emerge as the future unfolds. We must, however, be prepared.